Ancient Civilizations

THE INCA

by Elizabeth Andrews

An Imprint of Pop!
popbooksonline.com

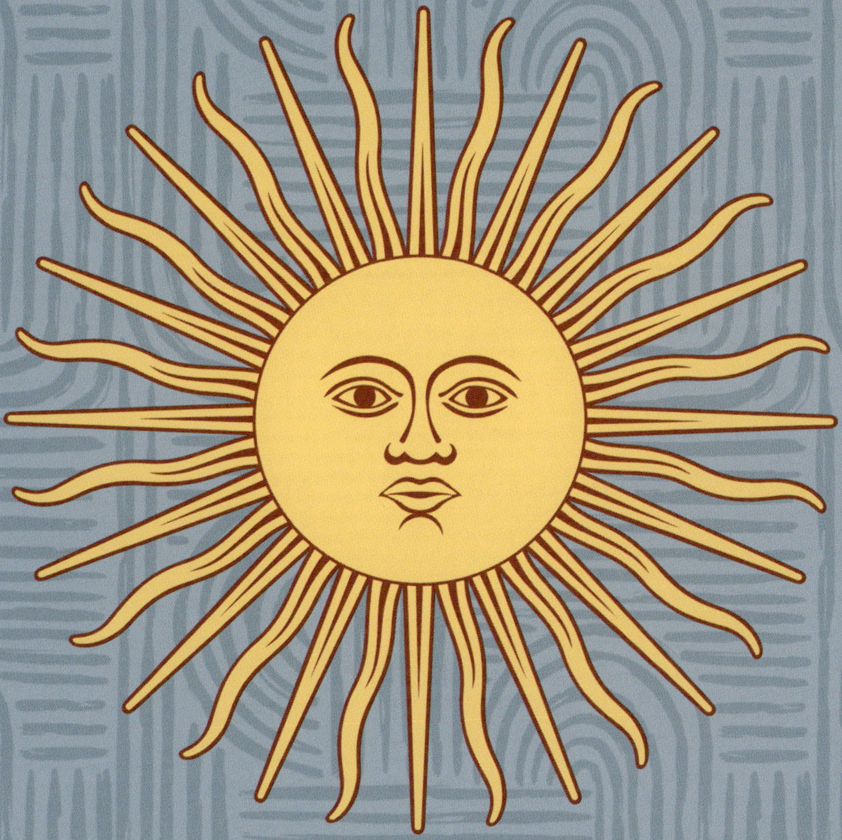

WELCOME TO DiscoverRoo!

This book is filled with videos, puzzles, games, and more! Scan the QR codes* while you read, or visit the website below to make this book pop.

popbooksonline.com/inca

abdobooks.com

Published by Pop!, a division of ABDO, PO Box 398166, Minneapolis, Minnesota 55439. Copyright © 2023 by Abdo Consulting Group, Inc. International copyrights reserved in all countries. No part of this book may be reproduced in any form without written permission from the publisher. DiscoverRoo™ is a trademark and logo of Pop!.

Printed in the United States of America, North Mankato, Minnesota.

102022
012023

THIS BOOK CONTAINS RECYCLED MATERIALS

Cover Photo: North Wind Picture Archives/Alamy Stock Photo, Shutterstock Images
Interior Photos: Shutterstock Images, Historia/Shutterstock, Universal History Archive/Shutterstock, CEllen/Wikimedia Commons, Gift and Bequest of Alice K. Bache, Stephanie Colasanti/Shutterstock, Cci/Shutterstock
Editor: Emily Dreher
Series Designer: Laura Graphenteen

Library of Congress Control Number: 2022941115

Publisher's Cataloging-in-Publication Data
Names: Andrews, Elizabeth, author.
Title: The Inca / by Elizabeth Andrews
Description: Minneapolis, Minnesota : Pop!, 2023 | Series: Ancient civilizations | Includes online resources and index.
Identifiers: ISBN 9781098243289 (lib. bdg.) | ISBN 9781098243982 (ebook)
Subjects: LCSH: Peru--History--Juvenile literature. | Inca Indians--Juvenile literature. | Ancient civilization--Juvenile literature. | Indigenous peoples--Social life and customs--Juvenile literature. | Cultural anthropology--Juvenile literature.
Classification: DDC 972.01--dc23

*Scanning QR codes requires a web-enabled smart device with a QR code reader app and a camera.

TABLE OF CONTENTS

CHAPTER 1
Rise and Fall..................... 4

CHAPTER 2
Incan Society.................... 10

CHAPTER 3
Life in the Empire 16

CHAPTER 4
Inca Religion 22

Making Connections.............. 30
Glossary 31
Index............................ 32
Online Resources 32

CHAPTER 1

RISE AND FALL

The first Inca were hunter-gatherers who traveled the Andes Mountains. Manco Capac was the first emperor of the Inca people. In the 1100s, the Inca settled in a valley. They named this new home Cuzco.

WATCH A VIDEO HERE!

The Inca had very advanced farming practices. For example, these steps built into this hill are called terraces.

The civilization spread from there. It ruled more than 12 million people who spoke 30 different languages.

Manco Capac, the first Inca emperor.

Starting in the 1300s, the Inca began invading other lands. In 1425, Emperor Viracocha proved how powerful the Inca were. He built a strong army that captured tribes south of Cuzco. The following emperors continued to take over new tribes through the Andes Mountains and surrounding valleys.

Sometimes the invaded tribes fought back, but Inca's emperors used their military well. They left soldiers in the places they **conquered**. The soldiers kept control of the captured land. Emperor Pachacuti knew that conquered people may start to **rebel**. Pachacuti forced certain tribes to move from their homes. This kept them from getting organized enough to fight back.

DID YOU KNOW? The Inca didn't leave any written records. Their early history is full of legends.

When the 11th emperor of the Inca died, his sons Huáscar and Atahuallpa argued over which one of them should get the throne. A **priest** told them to split the empire. One could rule the north. One could rule the south. But the brothers started a **civil war** for total power. They fought the biggest military battle in Inca history. Atahuallpa won in 1532.

During the civil war, Francisco Pizarro lead a group of Spaniards into the Inca empire. They carried European diseases that killed many Inca.

After the civil war, Pizarro invited Atahuallpa and his army to a feast. But it was a trick. The Spanish killed the army and captured Atahuallpa. Even after money and treasures were given, Pizarro still killed Atahuallpa. This marked the fall of the Inca empire.

Atahuallpa, the last Inca Emperor.

CHAPTER 2
INCAN SOCIETY

The Inca ruled millions of people throughout their empire. The **conquered** people were of different backgrounds and spoke different languages. People who spoke the Inca language had more privileges than ones who couldn't.

LEARN MORE HERE!

Today, a statue of Pachacuti can be seen in Cuzco, Peru.

Cuzco was the capital city. The emperors lived there with the royal family. The emperor oversaw all parts of life in the empire. A **priest** and ten trusted groups of **nobles** related to the emperor served as a council. They helped the

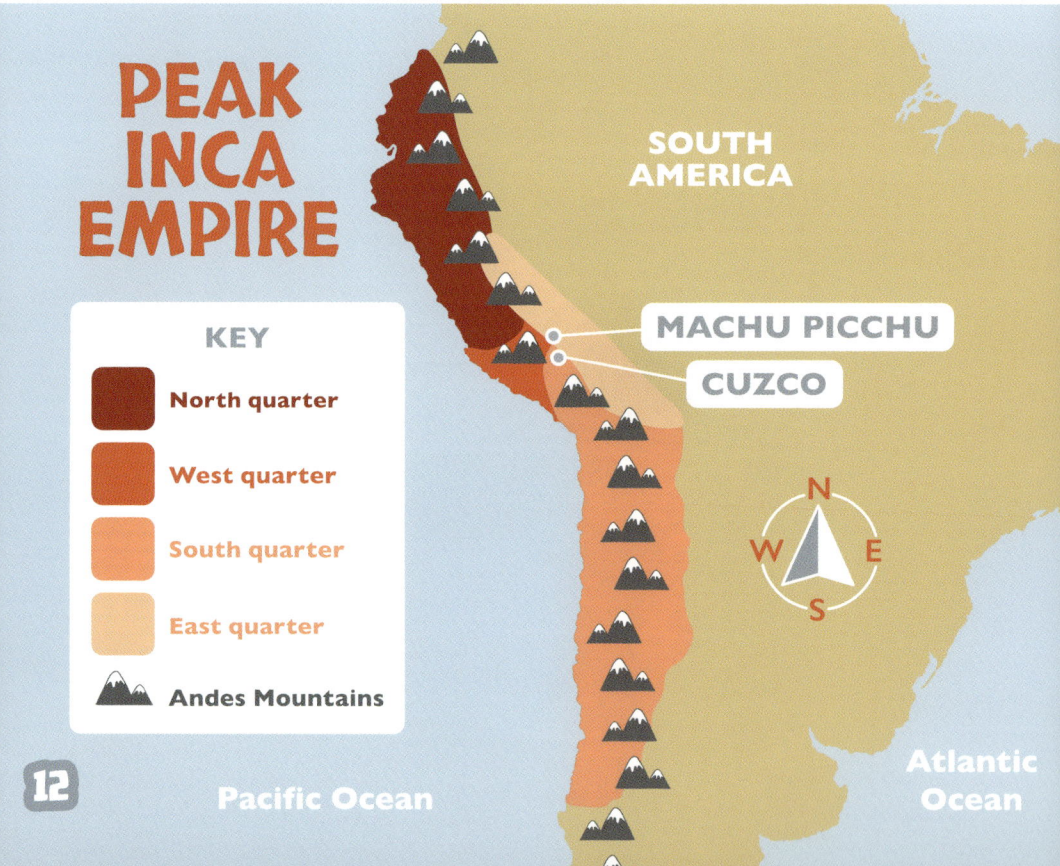

emperor make decisions. Inca who were distantly related to the emperor had power. There were also nobles who didn't have Inca blood.

    The Inca empire was divided into quarters. Each was ruled by a governor who reported to the emperor in Cuzco. The quarters were made up of smaller states that usually represented conquered tribes. Throughout the empire, government officials watched to make sure everyone followed the ways of the Inca.

Villages conquered by the Inca had to pay tributes. The tributes were mostly paid by fighting in the Inca's army, farming, and performing other services like engineering or arts.

Some tributes, such as pieces of art, were given to the Inca gods.

Llamas were the most important animals to the Inca. They provided food and wool for clothing.

Farmers gave two-thirds of their crop to the empire. If people paid tributes and followed the empire's rules, they were taken care of. They got food, places to live, access to the roads, and protection from the military.

CHAPTER 3

LIFE IN THE EMPIRE

Family ties were very important to the Inca. People lived in communities called ayllus. Ayllus were large groups of extended families who shared belongings, homes, land, and food. Different ayllus had their own god that they worshipped as a group.

EXPLORE LINKS HERE!

Inca people lived in brick homes with thatched roofs. The homes had little besides sleeping mats, a stove, and baskets for storage.

A thatched roof is made out of woven plant material.

Inca built rope bridges to connect their famous roads.

The Inca were powerful because all citizens worked for the good of the empire. Commoners worked harder than the **nobles**. Commoners were farmers, craftsmen, builders, and engineers.

Farmers were the largest group. They were also the poorest. But farmers' hard work kept everyone in the empire fed. Men and women worked on the farms. Women were also in charge of meals, caring for children, and making clothes.

ROADS AND RUNNERS

The Inca built more than 15,000 miles (24,140km) of roads to cover its empire. The roads were used to move people, food, and armies. Young, skilled runners sent information and messages throughout the empire. A runner would carry a message or package six to nine miles (10–15km) and then hand it off to another runner who was waiting for them. Together, 25 runners could cover 150 miles (240km) in a day!

Craftsmen made things like pottery, jewelry, and statues. Nobility paid them for their goods with food. Builders and engineers were also respected because they helped build the Inca's incredible cities and temples. They made these beautiful places without the basic technologies that most ancient civilizations had. The Inca did not have wheels or writing systems.

DID YOU KNOW? Machu Picchu is home to 300 houses, 50 other buildings, and man-made terraces for crops.

The Inca were excellent stonemasons. They built huge structures by fitting together stones without using **mortar**. Their building skills also made them great city planners. The layout of Cuzco was created to look like a puma from above. Some Inca roads and buildings can still be used today.

The perfect way Inca stones fit together keeps them from collapsing during earthquakes.

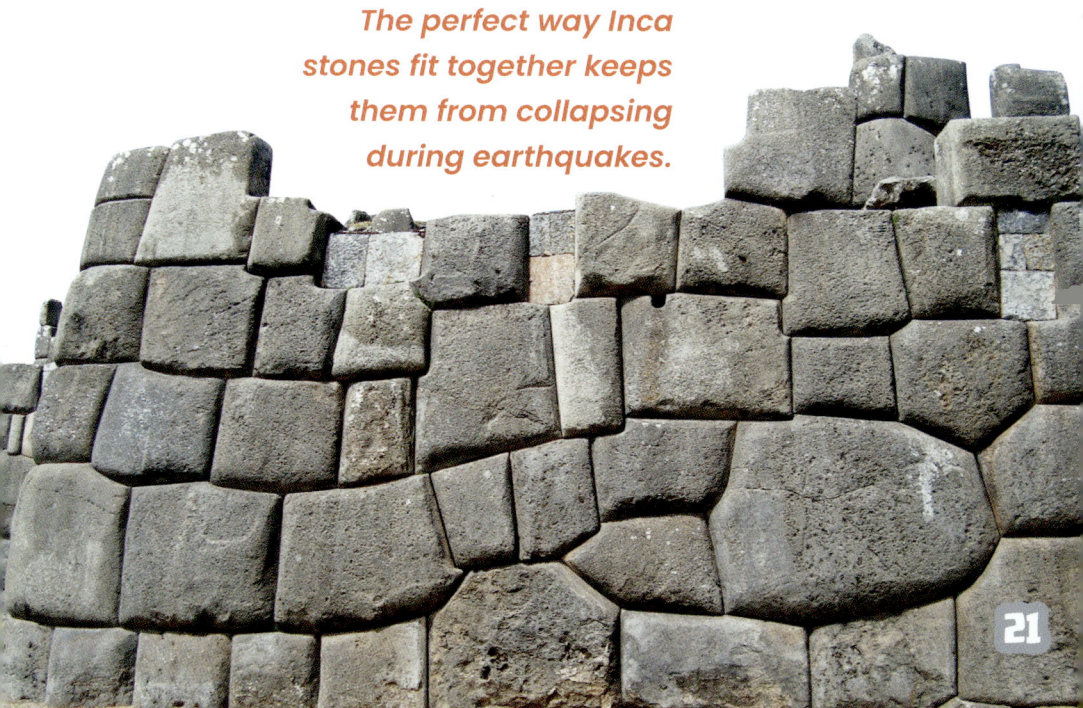

CHAPTER 4
INCA RELIGION

The Inca worshipped many gods. Life in the empire centered on the gods and their worship. The Inca believed the gods caused any good thing or bad thing to happen. So, they always worked hard to keep their gods happy.

COMPLETE AN ACTIVITY HERE!

The Inca believed gold was the blood of their sun god.

The god Viracocha was said to have created the sun, moon, heavens, Earth, and all living things. He was also the father of all other Inca gods.

Priests gave gifts to statues of their gods.

Inti was the Inca's most important god. He was the Sun God. He was believed to be the father of the original

Inca people. Inti was loved because his rays helped crops grow. The crops kept the Inca alive and well. Mama Quilla was Inti's wife. She was the Moon Mother.

Gods were worshipped at beautiful temples and **sacred** sites. **Priests** lived at temples and lead **ceremonies** on important days of the year. At ceremonies, they would make **sacrifices** to the gods with food and animals.

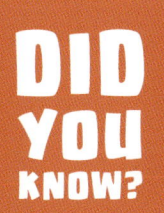

DID YOU KNOW? Human sacrifices were made during times of trouble such as droughts, royal deaths, and **eclipses**.

Since Inti was the most important, the Inca built him a beautiful temple called Coricancha. The temple was filled with gold. Its walls were crusted with emeralds. And it had a garden filled with corn fields and life-size animal statues all made from gold and silver.

People of the empire valued their ancestors. When important members of a community died, they were **mummified**. Mummies were put in sacred places. Sometimes Inca took mummies from their resting places and brought them to important events. They were dressed up and given their own food and drink.

The Andes Mountains' climate is perfect for preserving mummies. It is very dry and cold.

The Inca were the final civilization of South America before Europeans arrived. Even though they fell to the Spanish and left no written records, their traditions still

Machu Picchu is a famous site in the mountains near Cuzco. About 2,500 people visit it a day. To make the buildings, people had to push massive stones up the steep mountainside.

exist in the people of the Andes today. About 45 percent of Peru's population are descendants of the Inca. They left a beautiful mark on the world.

MAKING CONNECTIONS

TEXT-TO-SELF

How do you think the Inca were able to build such a beautiful place like Machu Picchu without wheels and iron tools?

TEXT-TO-TEXT

Have you read any other books about ancient civilizations that existed in South America? If so, what did they have in common with the Inca?

TEXT-TO-WORLD

Do you think it is a good or bad thing Machu Picchu gets thousands of visitors a day? Please explain your answer.

GLOSSARY

ceremony — a formal event or ritual held on a special occasion.

civil war — a war between groups in the same region.

conquer — to gain land by force.

eclipse — when one object in outer space blocks another from view.

mortar — a workable paste that hardens to bind building blocks such as stones, bricks, and concrete.

mummify — to turn a dead body into a mummy by preserving it with chemicals.

noble — a person of high rank or title.

priest — a person who oversees ceremonies, prayers, and offerings to the gods.

rebel — to resist authority.

sacred — connected with worship of a god.

sacrifice — a person or animal killed as an offering to please a god.

INDEX

Andes Mountains, 4, 7, 12, 29
Atahuallpa, 8–9
ayllus, 16

builders, 18, 20–21

Coricancha, 26
Cuzco, 4, 6, 12–13, 21

farmers, 14–15, 18–19

gods and goddesses, 22–25
government, 12–13

Huáscar, 8

languages, 5, 10

Manco Capac, 4
mummy, 26

Pachacuti, 7
Pizarro, Francisco, 8–9

roads, 15, 19, 21

sun, 23–24

tributes, 14–15

Viracocha (emperor), 6

DiscoverRoo!
ONLINE RESOURCES

This book is filled with videos, puzzles, games, and more! Scan the QR codes* while you read, or visit the website below to make this book pop.

popbooksonline.com/inca

*Scanning QR codes requires a web-enabled smart device with a QR code reader app and a camera.